Starts

GEYSERS

Claire Llewellyn

Heinemann Library
Chicago, Illinois

© 1998 Reed Educational & Professional Publishing
Published by Heinemann Interactive Library,
an imprint of Reed Educational & Professional Publishing,
Chicago, IL

Customer Service 888-454-2279

Visit our website at www.heinemannlibrary.com

Designed by David Oakley
Illustrations by Hardlines (p. 8) and Jo Brooker
Printed by Wing King Tong, in Hong Kong

06 05 04 03 02
10 9 8 7 6 5 4 3 2 1

Library of Congress Cataloging-in-Publication Data
Llewellyn, Claire.
     Geysers / Claire Llewellyn.
        p. cm. – (Geography starts)
     Includes bibliographical references (p.) and index.
     Summary: Explores the phenomenon of geysers, discussing their relationship with volcanic activity, the mechanics
of how a geyser works, steam vents, hot springs, and mud pots.
        ISBN 1-57572-204-6 (lib. bdg.)   ISBN 1-58810-972-0 (pbk. bdg.)
     1. Geysers—Juvenile literature. [1. Geysers.] I. Title. II. Series.
GB1198.5.L554 2000
551.2'3—dc21
                                    99-053325

Acknowledgments
The Publishers would like to thank the following for permission to reproduce photographs:
Bruce Coleman/Gunter Ziesler, p. 18; FLPA/David Hosking, pp. 7, 10, 11; FLPA/Winifried Wisniewski, p. 12;
NASA/Johnson Space Center, pp. 22, 24; Oxford Scientific Films/Stan Osolonski, p. 4; Oxford Scientific Films/James
Robinson, p. 5; Oxford Scientific Films/T. Middleton, p. 6; Oxford Scientific Films/Richard Packwood, p. 9; Oxford
Scientific Films/Norbert Rosing, p. 28; Peter Arnold Inc./Jim Wark, p. 26; Still Pictures/Hjalte Tin, pp. 13, 16; Still
Pictures/Jim Wark, p. 14; Still Pictures/B. & C. Alexander, p. 15; Still Pictures/Yves Thonnerieux, p. 17; Still Pictures/Steve
Kaufman, p. 19; Still Pictures/Massimo Lupioi, p. 20; Still Pictures/Andre Maslennieov, p. 21; Telegraph Color
Library/V.C.L., p. 29.

Cover photograph reproduced with permission of Robert Harding Picture Library.

Some words are shown in bold, **like this**. You can find
out what they mean by looking in the glossary.

Contents

What Is a Geyser?

A geyser is a **jet** of boiling water and steam that **erupts** out of the ground. It can shoot high up into the air.

This geyser shoots boiling water as high as an eight-story building.

Geysers look like holes in the ground when they are not erupting.

Most geysers last for a few minutes and then sink back down to the ground. Some geysers erupt again a few minutes or hours later. Others may not erupt for weeks, or longer.

Where to Find Geysers

Geysers are found where there is **volcanic activity**. There are geysers in New Zealand, Iceland, Russia, and the United States.

The word geyser means "rush forth."

Old Faithful erupts about once an hour.

Old Faithful is a geyser in Yellowstone **National Park** in Wyoming. Many people go there to watch it **erupt.**

How Are G ysers Mad ?

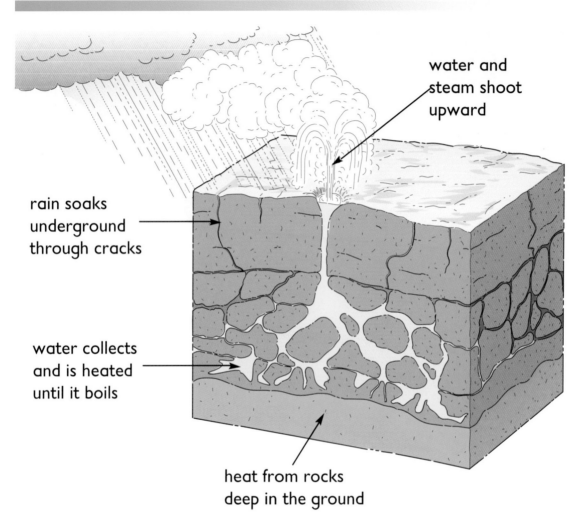

water and steam shoot upward

rain soaks underground through cracks

water collects and is heated until it boils

heat from rocks deep in the ground

The water in a geyser starts as rain. The rain runs down through cracks in the ground and collects in spaces between the rocks.

Bubbling, boiling water shoots
up out of the ground.

Near **volcanoes**, the rocks are very hot.
The water underground begins to boil. It
bubbles up through cracks in the rock and
erupts as a geyser.

From Water to Stone

Underground, the hot water **dissolves** the rock around it. Because of this, geyser water contains many tiny pieces of rock called **minerals**.

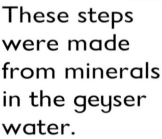

These steps were made from minerals in the geyser water.

Minerals can form many different shapes.

Above the ground, the geyser water cools. The small pieces of rocks and minerals are left behind and pile up on the ground. As the air cools them, they harden and become rock again.

G ysers in Ic land

There are many geysers in Iceland. Much of Iceland is covered with ice, but underground there is a lot of **volcanic activity**.

Iceland is known as a land of "fire and ice."

Sometimes, the geysers can **erupt** onto the ice. Then the hot water melts the ice. Streams of water pour downhill and can cause floods.

This much water may be dangerous for the people living on the flatland below.

Hot Springs

In some places, the hot water under the ground does not boil and shoot out as a geyser. It flows out more gently as a **hot spring**. The ground nearby is sometimes very brightly colored, because the springs are full of **minerals**.

Hot springs run into this **pool** in Yellowstone **National Park**.

These people are soaking in a hot spring in Iceland.

Some people think that the minerals in hot springs are like medicine for their muscles and bones. They soak in the springs to feel better.

Steam and Mud

Hot steam is formed where there is **volcanic activity**.

In some places near **hot springs** and geysers, small clouds of steam hiss out of the ground.

In other places, steam and hot water bubble up through a layer of clay. The water and clay mix together to make a hot mud **pool**.

This bubbling, hot mud pool is in Iceland.

Winter Warmth

Water from geysers and **hot springs** is always warm. This keeps nearby rivers and **pools** from freezing. Birds can feed there all winter long.

Canada geese feed on water plants in this pool near a geyser.

These **macaque** monkeys spend a lot of time sitting in hot springs.

In the mountains of Japan, the winters are very cold. Monkeys can keep themselves warm by sitting in the **hot springs.**

Using Geysers

Geysers give us **energy** that we can use. The hot water can be piped to swimming pools and homes. It can be used to heat **greenhouses.**

These bananas are growing in a greenhouse in Iceland.

The **jet** of steam helps to drive the machines.

A geyser's hot steam can be used to make **electricity.** It is a clean and cheap way to get power. This power station in Iceland makes electricity from nearby geysers.

Geyser Map 1

This photo shows a part of Yellowstone **National Park**. It was taken from a **satellite**. You can see Yellowstone Lake in the middle. The high mountains around the lake are covered with snow.

Key
lake
lowland
mountains

Maps are pictures of the land. This map
shows us the same place as the photo. The
blue color shows the lake. The wiggly lines
show the mountains.

Geyser Map 2

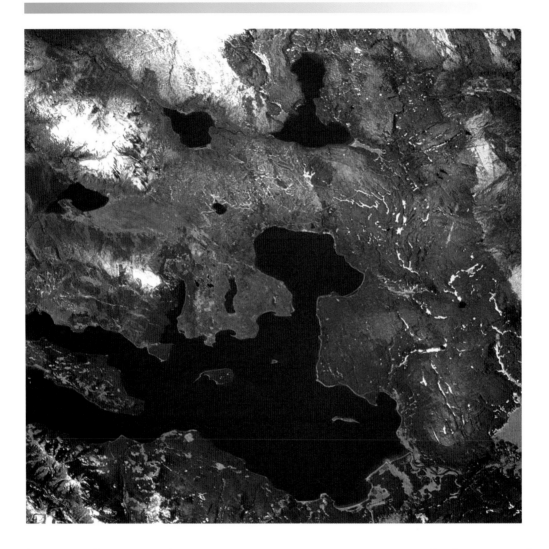

This photo shows a smaller area of the park. You can see Yellowstone Lake in the middle. You can also see a river flowing into the lake at the bottom right of the picture.

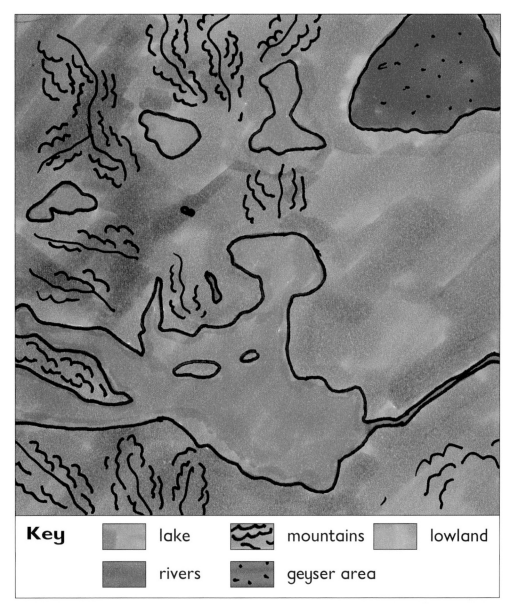

Key		lake		mountains		lowland
		rivers		geyser area		

The key on the map tells us what the colors mean. The river is easy to see on the map. It is a thin green line. The purple blob shows the area where the geysers and **hot springs** are.

Geyser Map 3

This photo shows the geyser area of Yellowstone **National Park**. It was taken from an airplane. You can see the bright colors of the **hot springs**. They are in the area where the geysers **erupt**.

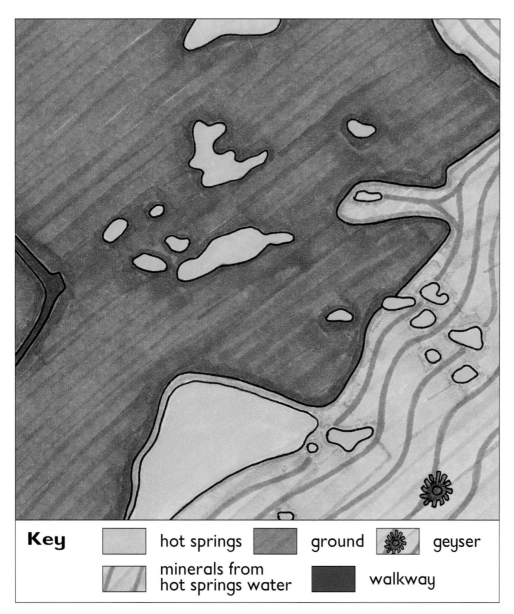

Key		hot springs		ground		geyser
		minerals from hot springs water		walkway		

The hot springs are colored blue. The **minerals** that have come out of the hot springs are shown with green and orange stripes. On the left of the map, you can see a walkway where people can watch the geyser.

Amazing Geyser Facts

When Old Faithful **erupts,** it shoots out a **jet** of boiling water that is two times as high as the Washington Monument!

This is Mount Tarawera now.

The highest-ever geyser was near Mount Tarawera in New Zealand. It once shot up higher than the Sears Tower—that's the tallest building in the United States!

Glossary

dissolve to disappear in water

electricity power that makes appliances, such as lights, televisions, and radios, work

energy ability or power to do work

erupt to suddenly shoot out hot water and steam

greenhouse building made of glass where plants can be grown in cold weather

jet very strong stream of water or steam

hot spring warm water that bubbles gently up out of the ground

macaque kind of short-tailed monkey (You say muh-kahk.)

mineral hard, tiny grain from which rocks are made

national park land that is protected by law to keep it safe and beautiful

pool pond of water that has been made by water coming out of the ground and not by man

satellite special machine that goes around the earth in space taking photographs of the earth

volcanic activity melting of rocks deep in the earth that causes gas to rise and make holes in the ground

volcano hill or mountain made by hot rocks that come out of an opening in the earth

More Books to Read

Armentrout, Patricia. *Hot Springs & Geysers*. Vero Beach, Fla.: Rourke Press, Incorporated, 1996.

An older reader can help you with these books:

Bryan, T. Scott. *Geysers: What They Are & How They Work*. Niwot, Colo.:Rinehart, Roberts Publishers, 1990.

Gallant, Roy A. *Geysers: When Earth Roars*. Danbury, Conn.: Franklin, Watts, 1997.

Index